Concussion Transformation

Overcoming the #1 Silent, Secret Killer of Relationships, Careers, and Lives

Kevin Donahue

Concussion Transformation

Published by:
90-Minute Books
302 Martinique Drive
Winter Haven, FL 33884
www.90minutebooks.com

Published in the United States of America

ISBN-13: 978-0692626368
ISBN-10: 0692626360

For more information on 90-Minute Books including finding out how you can
publish your own lead generating book, visit www.90minutebooks.com or call
(863) 318-0464

Here's What's Inside…

Foreword

Concussions are not just something that affects athletes. There are over 3.5 million reported and documented concussions in the United States every single year. Conservative estimates suggest that, in actuality, only one out of every five concussions are actually reported, and 90% of those reported are not Sport related. What is even more staggering is that 650,000 more people each year will have persistent symptoms unresponsive to traditional care.

For thousands of years, since the Ancient Greek and Roman days, concussions have been overlooked. Getting your bell rung, seeing stars, taking one for the team, and many other euphemisms have been created to casually discuss one of the most significant, accumulative, and debilitating conditions known to mankind today; a traumatic brain injury. In just a split second a concussion can change your entire life. It can take you from happy to depressed, calm to anxious, vibrant to bed-stricken. In the blink of an eye, people experience on remitting headaches, neck pain, fatigue, sensitivity to light and sound, and fogginess. Just one bump on the head can make a person's heart race, make them feel disconnected from their body, paralyzed, or even neglect one half of the world.

The brain has one sole purpose: to interact with the world for survival. Whenever the brain is injured, even the simplest things in life become complex and exhausting. It's never "just a concussion". I feel that I've been given the blessing of a lifetime to develop an understanding of the brain, how it is injured, and how it heals. Each day I am in awe at the marvel of neuroplasticity, or the brain's ability to learn and heal when given proper cognitive and physical exercises. Every day, I learn from and am inspired by my patients, their stories, their hope, and their strength to persevere. I hope that this story of one individuals tenacious journey to recovery installs hope, and guides you or someone that you love, back to a life of maximal potential. It's only 7 steps away!

Matthew Antonucci, DC, DACNB, FACFN, FICC

Director of Neurological Performance and Rehabilitation at Plasticity Brain Centers

Introduction

How I Recovered from Post-Concussion Syndrome in 7 Simple Steps

September 15, 2015
Phoenix, AZ

My name is Kevin Donahue, and I'm a concussion survivor. I've gone through the hell of post-concussion syndrome and have lived to tell you about it! I've written this book to share some of the insights and breakthroughs I've gained through my own personal experience, suffering from and recovering from a concussion.

I've actually had several concussions in my lifetime, but this time, the time that inspired this book to be written, almost ruined my life! It's my hope that by reading this, you will find hope and inspiration on your own road to recovery.

Before going through my suffering, I did not understand why veterans and famous football players committed suicide at numbers so high that they far outpace casualties on the battlefield. I did not understand what people who had suffered brain injures dealt with on a day-to-day basis and how horrific their struggles were. By going through the hell of it and coming out the other side, I soon discovered that job loss, divorce, alcoholism, and suicide are just side effects of dealing with a brain that has been injured.

This book is designed to give you some insights from my personal experiences of suffering from a mild traumatic brain injury (concussion). I will be using the terms "traumatic brain injury" and "concussion" interchangeably throughout this book. I will also often use the acronym MTBI when discussing mild traumatic brain injury and PCS when discussing post-concussion syndrome.

Over the next few pages, I am going to share with you intimate details of my tragedy, some insights into the struggling and suffering that I went through, what I did to help speed up my recovery time, and the triumph over my challenges. I will even share what I still struggle with today. What I have learned from my personal experiences has opened my eyes to the world of brain injuries and the suffering that is taking place every moment in our world today. From my experience, my amateur research, and the conversations I've had, I have come to believe that post-concussion syndrome (PCS), also known as mild traumatic brain injury (MTBI), is the number-one silent, secret killer of careers, relationships, dreams, and lives. Keep reading, and I'll tell you why.

Most injuries that people deal with that are physical in nature are fairly obvious when they happen. If you were to sprain your ankle, for instance, you would see swelling; feel pain; and perhaps have limited mobility, maybe walking with a limp. You would know right away that you had an injury! Others could clearly see it too, and you could seek medical attention if necessary. If you broke your arm, you would know something was wrong, doctors would X-ray the injured area, and they would put your arm in a cast and order you to stop any activity that could cause further injury.

The biggest challenge of a concussion is that it often goes unnoticed and undiagnosed because it is not an injury that can be seen by an outside observer, and it cannot be felt by the person who has suffered the injury. If you were to see a bloody gash or an obvious break in the skin, you would deal with the injury immediately; the person suffering would be reeling in pain.

Concussions, however, are often silent and go unnoticed. They occur when you fall off your bike or skateboard and bang your head (even if you're wearing a helmet). They occur when you are playing a competitive sport and collide with your opponent or teammate, or when you are in an automobile accident and walk away fine but never take into consideration that your brain may have been injured. In all of these cases, you get up, brush yourself off, and go on living your life as planned, without taking into consideration the trauma your sensitive brain may have undergone.

As I've heard Dr. Daniel Amen say in his PBS shows and in his talks, "...the brain is the consistency of warm butter in our skulls, and when we are abruptly stopped or fall or are in accidents, our sensitive brains bump up against the hard, boney ridges of the skull and cause bruising and damage." Even minor falls or collisions can cause the brain to be bruised, and while science has taught us so much about the brain and the nervous system, the brain is still a vast, unexplored universe and a complex mystery. Even the slightest injury can have major effects on the person who was injured, and it may manifest differently in each person. The challenge is still that the brain injury cannot be seen without very special and expensive equipment, and the victim of a brain injury can't feel it either.

This leaves the person with an injury that they don't know about and for which they never get treated. Then they suffer the debilitating effects of PCS or MTBI, which can include:

- Depression
- Personality changes
- Anxiety attacks
- Confusion
- Emotional outbursts
- Headaches
- Dizziness
- Fatigue
- Memory problems
- Vertigo
- Irritability
- Sensitivity to light
- Trouble concentrating
- Difficulty in social situations

While the rest of the world goes on as it did before, someone suffering from PCS is left to cope with newfound problems that they don't understand and others don't understand either. Since both the victim of the brain injury and the people around them don't know about the brain injury, the suffering goes on silently.

People with PCS often become withdrawn or act out in ways they never have before. I've heard of people who suddenly suffer panic attacks in situations that are normal to them, like standing in line at a grocery store or driving a car down a road they've traveled hundreds of times before. They are often unable to complete menial tasks at their jobs or complete normal chores around their houses. They become more irritable or get fatigued in situations that normally wouldn't cause them to be tired.

All of this occurs with no explanation to them. If someone had a sprained ankle, others would know why they weren't playing basketball or going to the gym to walk on the treadmill. They would be sympathetic and empathetic because they would understand that the person had an injury. The challenge with PCS is that there are no physical signs of injury, and victims look exactly how they did prior to the incident. Nonetheless, they feel as if, and often look to the outside world as if, they are going crazy. In a sense, they are, but it's not their fault; they are silently suffering from an injury to the organ that controls their lives: the brain.

What you will discover in this report is what it is like to suffer from a concussion or MTBI through my personal experience, and you'll gain some insights into how you might be able to spot this disease in yourself or others. I will also share intimate details of my accident, what it was like going through life for several weeks not knowing that I was suffering from a brain injury, how I discovered I had a brain injury, and what I did to help myself recover. I will reveal symptoms, personality shifts, emotional breakdowns, my pain and suffering, and how I was able to find the resources to get myself well.

In my sharing, I hope you find some gold nuggets of wisdom that you can use in your life or apply to the life of a loved one to help them find the help they need. I will share the resources I used, the supplements I took, the diet changes I made, the community I created, and my general road to recovery. I hope this special report moves you to take action in your life to protect your brain and the brains of your loved ones, and I hope with all my heart that you find the healing you need. My goal is to help you and those around you recover from the silent, secret killer of relationships, careers, and lives. I want you to find healing for your brain and for your life!

First, this very special message from the disclaimer department.

Very Important Disclaimer—Please Read!

No Advice

This document contains general information about medical conditions and treatments used by the author. The information is not advice and should not be treated as such.

Limitation of Warranties

The information in this report is provided "as is" without any representations or warranties, express or implied. The Author makes no representations or warranties in relation to the information in this report.

Professional Assistance

You must not rely on the information in this document as an alternative to medical advice from your doctor or other professional healthcare provider.

Disclaimer Continues...

If you have any specific questions about any medical matter, you should consult your doctor or other professional healthcare provider.

If you think you may be suffering from any medical condition, you should seek immediate medical attention.

You should never delay seeking medical advice, disregard medical advice, or discontinue medical treatment because of information in this document.

Now that you understand that this is simply my story and my experience and that I am not a doctor and don't hope to be one, I would like to share with you what happened to me.

The Incident:

December 28, 2012

1:00 PM

90 degrees F and sunny

Montañita, Ecuador

On December 28, 2012, I was enjoying a spectacular motorcycle ride up the coastal highway just north of the beautiful beach city of Montañita, Ecuador. The waves were too choppy for surfing that day, and my friend Anthony and I decided it was a great day to see the countryside.

We rented 100cc off-road motorbikes and took off up the highway for an inland adventure. As we cruised up the curving highway, we passed through towns and up and down hills, enjoying the scenery and often passing slow-moving vehicles.

I then saw a box truck slowing to a stop and making a left turn on a side road. I sped up to pass him on the right, but the truck turned right! The driver's apparent left-hand turn was just him steering to make a wider right-hand turn.

I instinctively let off the gas and pulled the handbrake as I pushed the foot break. The motorcycle began to screech and skid, but I had nowhere to go. My last thoughts were, "No, no, no! Stop, stop, STOP!"

Then, THUD! My front tire hit the truck first, and I flew headfirst into the passenger door of the truck. My body followed close behind, crumpling into the solid metal wall, and then I bounced off and onto the dirt and pavement. I lay there, dazed and confused. What had just happened?

There I was in a third-world country, far from home, far from any decent medical facility, no ability to call 9-1-1, lying in the street, conscious and aware that I had just been in a motorcycle wreck. The men from the truck got out briefly as I staggered up into a standing position. Then they quickly got back into their truck and left.

I looked down at the bent front wheel of the motorcycle, and as I lifted my left arm, I felt a searing pain shoot down it.

"AAAGH, I think it's broken!"

Luckily, Anthony, who had been about 50 yards behind me, was there to assist, and thankfully, I didn't appear to be hurt badly. I had been wearing a helmet and had slowed considerably by the time I hit the truck.

Suddenly, however, I became dizzy and nauseous. I lay back down and asked Anthony to find some ice for my arm. There was a home and a local store nearby, so I told him to get some *hielo* (ice).

I lay there in shock, waiting for Anthony to return, my mind racing about how I would repair my broken arm, how I would get back to Montañita, and how I had gotten myself into this mess. All of my thoughts were for my immediate survival, which I later understood is a natural and normal response to any tragic event.

Certain that my arm was broken, I did the only thing that I knew to do as I lay there: I prayed. I prayed for healing, I prayed for help, and I prayed that I would be okay. I knew that my injuries were not life-threatening, but I also knew that my blood was pumping full of adrenaline and that maybe I was suffering something more than I could see or feel. I also knew that there was no 9-1-1. No one was coming to rescue me; I was on my own to figure this situation out.

I was in pain; my motorcycle front wheel had been crushed; I was lying on the side of a highway in Ecuador; and little did I know, I had suffered a concussion. The sudden collision and my body slamming headfirst into the side of the truck caused my soft and sensitive brain to slam against my hard skull and bounce around inside my head. When I landed on the ground, my helmet struck with force, and my brain was jolted again. All I knew at that time, however, was that I had injured my arm.

After a little while, I was able to stand up, and Anthony and I walked across the highway to a home, where I rested, and the kind people offered drinks and food. After about an hour, we got onto Anthony's bike and rode back to the town where we had rented the motorcycles. Besides my arm throbbing in pain, I seemed to be okay.

The motorcycle shop sent out a repairman to pick up the bike and get an estimate of the damage, and then Anthony and I were off to find a hospital. We found an emergency room that could X-ray broken bones. They found nothing broken, prescribed me some pain medication, and we were on our way. They never even considered that I may have injured my brain.

Over the next couple of days, I noticed that I was very fatigued. I would become irritable. It seemed I needed a coffee every couple of hours. Then, on the morning of January 1, 2013, I woke up, and I knew I had to get out of Ecuador.

I was up at 5:00 AM and decided to catch the bus from Montañita to the airport in Guayaquil to fly home. During the entire two- to three-hour bus ride, I was angry. I was angry at everyone and everything. I couldn't stop the anger. I tried to close my eyes and meditate, I tried to pray, I tried to think of things I was grateful for, I even tried to journal, but nothing worked. I was on TILT!

When I arrived at the bus station near the airport, I got off the bus and started walking to the taxis to take me to the airport. After stopping to use the restroom, I realized that I had forgotten to get my bag off the bus! I started to think I was going a little bit crazy. I thought, "Who leaves their luggage behind when they're traveling?"

I felt a little air-headed, which made me even more angry. I got to the airport and booked a flight to Miami. During the entire flight, I was angry, so angry that I couldn't sleep.

The Aftermath: Spiraling Down Into a Dark Abyss

I spent a couple of days in Miami and then decided to fly to the suburbs of Washington, D.C., where my parents and siblings live. Something inside me wanted to be home, wanted familiarity and unconditional love.

My father picked me up at the airport. I told him about my accident and that I had injured my arm but that everything was fine. I spent the next three days on my parents' couch and in bed, sleeping most of the day and suffering through spells of fevers. I wanted to get up and play with my nieces and nephews, but I simply couldn't muster the energy. I couldn't keep my eyes open. I figured that I had picked up a flu or sickness in Ecuador that my body was fighting off. Little did I know that my brain was deteriorating.

After three days in the comfort of home, I flew back to Scottsdale, Arizona, where I went on with life as normal, except that life was not normal at all. In fact, I spiraled day after day into a deeper depression. I didn't know what was wrong with me: I couldn't get out of bed, I couldn't find the energy to go to the gym, and I would try to focus and concentrate but felt hyperactive and frustrated.

I started eating poorly, and to cope with my depression, I watched TV late into the night. I found my self-addicted to reality shows like *Pawn Stars* and *American Pickers* on History®. I would lie in bed and eat hamburgers and French fries, watching these programs. I would walk my dog at night, be overcome with emotion, and start crying. I had never suffered from an anxiety attack in my life, but the simple act of driving to the store would send me into a panic and force me to pull my car over.

I thought I was going insane. I reached out to friends and family to talk through things, but none of it made sense. I tried to listen to motivational tapes and read books and the Bible, but nothing helped; I had no interest at all.

I started dating someone new, whom I had met at church, but it seemed that all of my conversations with her were focused on the negative. This was frustrating because I am generally a *very* positive thinker!

I had been regularly attending a men's group on Wednesday evenings at church, but I didn't feel like going. I dragged myself there, showed up late, sat in the corner, and didn't speak. I sulked.

Halfway through the meeting, I got a text from Mike Burns that said, "Smile ☺." I looked up, and he winked at me and smiled. I was clearly not my normal self. I usually contributed to the group, spoke my mind, and furthered the discussion, but now I felt paralyzed, miserable, and like I didn't want to be there at all.

After that first men's group, several people asked if I was alright and said I did not seem like my normal self. I simply brushed them off and told them that I was going through a rough spot. I attributed it to the "new year blues," but it was much, much worse.

I knew I was sad, I knew I was in a funk, I knew this wasn't normal behavior for me, but I didn't know that my brain was bruised and struggling to heal and repair itself. I had no idea that it was in a 24/7 state of panic, afraid that I might injure it further.

The next week was full of more of the same. I was depressed, I couldn't get any work done, I was exhausted, I was irritable.

During my first week back, I had met a wonderful woman in church and asked her out on a date. We went on a couple of dates, but my conversations seemed to be negative, and I would have to drink coffee in order to stay awake.

I felt desperate, confused, and truly uncertain about life. I had no motivation and could not see hope in the future. There were moments when I felt that life was not worth living anymore. One night I was walking my dog and began to cry. I had no idea why! I felt sad, but there was nothing obvious to be sad about; my emotional reaction was out of line with my life circumstances. I thought I was depressed.

That night I went online and started looking for a life coach. Thankfully, I had invested in my personal development and had taken courses such as The Landmark Forum, Tony Robbins' programs, and a course that would later prove to be very important called Lifebook. I had also read many books by Steven Covey, Zig Ziglar, and others in the personal development and self-help realms. Furthermore, I was deeply impacted by my Christian/Catholic faith upbringing, which helped me to search for hope in a world that seemed darkened.

At night I sat in my bed, watched TV, and ate comfort foods like hamburgers and French fries. This was very odd behavior for me; I had not watched TV in years, and I am very much invested in my health and bodybuilding. This new behavior, however, was my escape. Night after night I sat in my bed and watched marathons of History. I would watch six episodes in a row of *Pawn Stars* followed by four episodes of *American Pickers* until I fell asleep. For some reason, those shows comforted me; it felt like the characters were my friends. I also believe the novelty of each episode, during which they discover different things, held my interest.

Again, I knew I wasn't being my normal self. I was too exhausted to go to the gym, I was withdrawn and anti-social, and I was eating junk food and watching TV! I felt my life spinning out of control. My normal motivated, inspired, live-life-to-the-fullest self had surrendered to a couch potato. I fell deeper into a depression and had little hope for my future.

During the day, I scrolled through my phone and searched for people to call who might be able to cheer me up or give me some encouragement and insight that would lift me out of my funk. I was desperate, looking for anyone who could give me the slightest feeling of inspiration, but the more I spoke with people, the more I felt alone; I felt like I couldn't relate to anyone.

I tried to do work, but it took three hours for me to finish an email that would normally take three to five minutes. I would sit in a coffee shop and drink two to three cups of coffee just to make it through the morning.

I tried to attend an event with other entrepreneurs, but I couldn't sit still or pay attention. I attributed all of this to ADD or ADHD, but that didn't help me deal with my life.

Sometime in mid-January I was driving down the road and suffered from an extreme feeling of being overwhelmed. I had an anxiety attack. At that time, I had never suffered from anything like that before. I pulled my car over into a mall parking lot and cried. I eased my seat back to lie down and closed my eyes. I didn't want to go on living this way. I had gone from a strong, powerful man with vision and purpose to a crying, frantic mess. It had to come to an end.

I suffered through that next week and went to my men's group the next Wednesday evening. Again, I just sat and listened, not participating. At the end the leader asked for prayer requests. I raised my hand and said, "I need prayer for something, but I don't know what. I seem to have lost my direction and need prayer to help me find it again. I don't know what has happened, but I haven't been my normal self since the beginning of the year."

The leader of the group prayed and asked God for guidance and to give me healing and comfort. I left feeling no better than I had. I went home, picked up some comfort food, and started my routine of watching History until I fell asleep.

The following weekend I was invited by a friend to attend a marketing conference in San Francisco. I packed my things and flew out the next day, after my men's group.

Prior to my accident, I was the person who went to an event or conference and knew just about everyone. I engaged in powerful conversations with people, interacted with friends, and connected with new clients or partners.

This time I felt like doing none of that. I went from being an extravert to having no desire to speak with anyone. I just wanted to hide out. My entire identity had shifted.

I arrived at the hotel in San Francisco and immediately found a local hamburger restaurant. Afterwards, I bought chocolate bars from a convenience store. The friend who had invited me to the event asked if I was okay; he had noticed a subtle shift in my personality. I brushed it off.

The next day at the event, I could not sit still in the sessions. I thought about anything and everything except the topics being discussed. I challenged my friend sitting next to me to a game of tic-tac-toe I doodled in my notepad. I wanted to be anywhere but there.

During the first break, I was overwhelmed by the crowds, and the noise made it feel like I was in a cyclone of people. Old friends said hello, new people shook my hand, but none of it made sense. I was totally overwhelmed.

I fell deeper into a depression. I was spiraling down and did not know what to do about it. I could not explain what I was going through, and my emotions made no sense to me. I could not figure out what was wrong, so I hid my feelings from almost everyone. I suffered silently as my brain did the best it could to make sure I survived every day.

The Discovery!

I ran into an old friend, Alexandra, at the event and asked her if she wanted to grab breakfast the next morning. She agreed, and we met at a diner across from the hotel. I sat across from her and explained some of my distress, that I had lost direction, and that I might need a life coach. I needed a breakthrough!

We ordered our food, and she looked at me with concerned eyes as she began to talk about life and business. As our food was delivered, she said something that changed my life from that point forward.

Alexandra asked me if I had heard of Brendon Burchard and if I knew of the ATV accident he had been in while he was in Mexico. I mentioned that I had heard him speak of it, and she went on to say how he had suffered a concussion. When he returned from Mexico, he couldn't complete normal tasks and found himself in a dilemma because he had a book deadline.

I stopped Alexandra, grabbed her arms, and exclaimed, "That's it! You just saved my life! I have a brain injury!"

Alexandra smiled and said, "Well, I don't know if you have a brain injury or not, but that's what happened to Brendan."

I said, "No, no, no, you don't understand! During the motorcycle accident, I went headfirst into the truck, and I bounced off the ground after the truck. I have a brain injury!"

She giggled a bit and said jokingly, "Well, congratulations, you have a brain injury!"

My eyes were wide with excitement. I finally knew what was wrong with me! I had suffered a concussion during my accident and didn't know it. I couldn't see the injury or feel the injury, so I had no idea that I was injured. Still, I was walking around with a bruised and damaged brain; I was experiencing the results of a concussion.

I was beyond excited because I finally knew what was wrong with me. I was not suffering from some strange mid-life crisis, lack of direction, depression, or an illness that had zapped me of my strength. I had a brain injury! I was jumping for joy. The prayer I had said two days earlier, asking for help, had been answered!

I left the diner a changed man. Fortunately, I had studied the brain with an education company called Z-Health. I had listened to Dr. Daniel Amen and his wife Tana time and again give lectures on the brain, the effects of mild traumatic brain injuries, and how to recover. I had read Dr. Amen's book, *Change Your Brain, Change Your Life*. I had also read a book on neuroplasticity and how the brain is always changing. It all came together in that breakfast meeting when Alexandra alerted me to the possibility of a concussion.

I called the woman I was dating and let her know that she had never met the real me, that my brain had been injured, and I was suffering from the effects of a concussion. She understood and was relieved for me. I told my friends at the event, and they all instantly understood the change in my personality that they hadn't been able to figure out.

I flew back to Scottsdale with a newfound hope. A small light had broken through my world of darkness. When I arrived in Scottsdale, I immediately called my friend Joe Polish to share my discovery with him. He had known about my motorcycle accident and my arm injury but had no idea the suffering I had been silently enduring.

We met at his office, and I told him all that I had been going through and my symptoms, and I told him what Alexandra had shared about Brendon Burchard. Joe picked up his phone and called Brendan. We told Brendan what had happened to me, and he began to explain his post-concussion syndrome symptoms. One by one, he listed everything that I had been suffering through. Joe looked up, amazed that Brendon explained almost word-for-word what I was going through: inability to concentrate, inappropriate emotional responses, exhaustion, depression, anxiety, and more.

Joe texted his neuroscience doctor, and I booked an appointment with him the next day. He did an EEG-type scan on my brain and identified left frontal lobe damage and rear left damage. He explained to me that I had classic symptoms of mild traumatic brain injury or post-concussion syndrome. He gave me a short protocol of things to do and told me to rest. Beyond that, there was not much he could do; I was on my own. It was time for me to get well again.

Now I will share with you the seven-step process that got me back to health and back to an extraordinary life!

My 7 Steps to Recovery

Step 1: Awareness

The first step to recovering from a mild traumatic brain injury is to know that you have suffered one. This is much more difficult than it sounds. Because of the nature of a brain injury or concussion, you can't feel or see the injury. Often, those suffering from concussions brush off their falls or injuries and get back in the game, get back to work, and get back to normal activities.

When you first suffer a slight trauma to the head, you may experience a surge of adrenaline and be able to quickly bounce back. The effects of the concussion may not be noticed for several days. By that time, you've likely forgotten about the injury.

Remember the common misconception I mentioned earlier: If there's no blood or obvious swelling or pain, then nothing is wrong. This is *not* the case with a concussion. Therefore, realizing you have a concussion is the very first step. Once you know you've been injured, you can deal with the injury in a number of ways, but at least you can deal with it.

Continue on through my steps, and I will share with you my path to recovery.

Step 2: Being Gentle with Yourself

Once I realized I had a brain injury, I decided that in order for me to heal, I had to allow myself to take a step back from the activities in which I was involved. With everything from business to travel to sports, I simply had to be gentle with myself.

Prior to knowing I had a brain injury, I was trying to push through, force myself to do things, and be my old self. Once I realized that I had a brain injury, I began to treat myself like a five-year-old child who was sick and needed comfort, support, and encouragement. I allowed myself to not be a responsible adult, but to be a little boy in need of care. This was very helpful to me. Instead of getting upset with myself, I nurtured myself. I allowed myself to take naps when I needed them. When I had breakdowns, I thought of a child having a temper tantrum. I just smiled and said to myself, "It will be alright, little guy."

Having that persona in my mind created a space between myself and my emotional responses to the world. It proved to be very valuable. Therefore, in Step 2 I urge you to be forgiving of not being who you were prior to your accident. Be accommodating to your inner little boy or girl, try to smile in the midst of a breakdown, and care for yourself as if you were a child.

Step 3: Being Open to Sharing with Others and Creating a Powerful, Positive Environment

This step was critical to my survival and for thriving during my time with an injured brain! I shared with everyone that I had suffered a brain injury from a motorcycle accident in Ecuador.

First, I called my parents, who lived in Virginia. I told them that I was suffering and would need them to check in on me and tell me they loved me more often than usual. I called my brothers and sisters, my friends, and my colleagues and let them all know that I wasn't my normal self and that I would need their patience and love. I told women that my suffering was similar to severe PMS symptoms, but instead of about once a month, I experienced them every day. I was on an emotional roller coaster with seemingly no direction and no end in sight. When I met new people or was invited to dinner or an appointment, I shared with the person or people there that I was suffering from post-concussion syndrome and that they shouldn't worry if I needed to get up and be alone for a moment.

Everyone was very accommodating, and my sharing often led to invitations to luncheons and alternative therapies, recommendations of books, and even the sharing of personal stories of PCS. Everyone was very understanding and concerned, but no one really knew what I was going through. I still suffered silently in my mind, but at least others now knew what was going on.

This step was critical to my healing. Being open to sharing with others and entering a conversation about what I was dealing with proved to be very powerful for me and my recovery.

It is also very important to surround yourself with positive people and avoid people who are negative or draining. In my case, I was very emotionally sensitive, and even the slightest negative energy could send me into a negative tailspin. Where before I had an abundance of energy to give and share, during my recovery, I struggled to find it in me to contribute to others. This was hard for me because I have always identified myself as a giver. It was important for me to allow myself to receive love, support, and friendship from others. The outpouring of support I received from friends, family, and even strangers was truly amazing.

It was also important for me to turn off the news and anything else that was negative so that I could maintain a positive outlook on my recovery.

Step 4: Nutrition

Nutrition became a critical part of my recovery. Thankfully, I had always been healthy and had also taken supplements, but now I had a specific goal: Get my brain healthy again.

I listened again to Dr. Daniel Amen's audiobook, *Change Your Brain, Change Your Life*, to get a better understanding of what supplements could help me with recovery and what kind of diet is most beneficial to the brain. I had heard Dr. Amen speak at events and on PBS, so I was familiar with his protocols for brain recovery. I had also read his published report about NFL football players and how they could improve their brains with smart nutrition, supplements, and better lifestyle choices.

I embarked on a very purposeful diet, which included natural foods that were high in fats and protein. I drank a lot of water and limited the amount of refined sugars I consumed. I took what seemed like handfuls of supplements, including fish oils, multivitamins, and neuro-specific supplements.

Below is a list of what I consumed. As the disclaimer mentioned, I am not a doctor or medical professional. I am simply a guy who got into a motorcycle accident, suffered a concussion, and found healing for myself. I highly recommend that you see your doctor or medical professional to find the diet and supplements that best fit your body and your situation.

Foods high in fats: Avocados; almonds; cashews; chia seeds; coconut oil; pumpkin seeds; egg yolks; peanut butter; natural oils; and other foods that have good, healthy fats.

Foods high in protein: Fish, chicken, bison burgers, eggs, protein powders

Foods high in good carbohydrates: Plain oatmeal; rice; fruits like blueberries, blackberries, raspberries, bananas, and more

Liquids: Lots of water, coconut water

Supplements: High-quality fish oil with a high EPA ratio, CLA, evening primrose oil, CoQ10, acetyl-L-carnitine, alpha lipoic acid, Phosphosidoserene, vitamin C, vitamin D, vitamin E, vitamin B complex, and a high-quality multivitamin twice per day

I highly recommend reading Dr. Daniel Amen's book, *Change Your Brain, Change Your Life*, to get a list of other supplements that have been shown to help improve brain function and for more specifics.

During my period of recovery (and to this day), I avoided alcohol, highly processed foods, refined sugars, and foods high in artificial colors and sweeteners.

Step 5: Rest

During my recovery, there were times in the day when I was utterly exhausted. During these moments, I found places to lie down and rest or take a nap. When I was in my office, I would find a quiet room and just close my eyes and rest. I made it okay for me to nap. I treated myself like a young boy who needed naptime a couple of times per day.

I found this to be very helpful. It also helped me deal with anxiety.

Step 6: Having Something Awesome to Look Forward To

I have a theory that life is better when we have something exciting to look forward to. I've always made a habit of putting cool things on my calendar that are a few months out. They make me work hard in the moment and focus on the exciting thing in the future.

For me, this is usually travel. When I was suffering from PCS, it was hard to get through a single day, so planning for tomorrow or for something in the future seemed virtually impossible. However, prior to my accident, I had been invited to attend a mastermind retreat for entrepreneurs on Necker Island, Richard Branson's private island in the Caribbean. The dates were April 7 to 16, but I did not want to be on the retreat in the condition that I was in. I needed to have my brain back by the time I stepped foot on that island, so I was committed to my own healing! I was willing to do whatever it took to get myself to a healthy place in order to be back to my old self in time for that trip. Anything the medical professionals told me, I would do.

Imagine for a moment that you are a professional baseball player, and your team has made it to the World Series. Imagine that you sustained an ankle injury during the end of the regular season. This is your first—and maybe only—time to play in a World Series game! Believe me, you would do everything you could to rehabilitate that ankle and get yourself back in playing shape to get in that game.

I believe this is a critical aspect of the healing process, especially with a brain injury. If you are suffering now or know of someone who is dealing with PCS, come up with something amazing, and put it on the calendar for a few months out. Don't make it right away because that may cause too much stress. Schedule it three to six months in the future, so it gives them something to look forward to!

Step 7: Serving Others

I have another theory: I believe that when we help others in need, especially if their situations are direr than our own, we begin to heal faster. There is something about helping others that lifts our spirits and causes us to focus less on our own challenges and more on the challenges of others.

During my recovery, I knew that I had to get out of my everyday environment and put myself in an environment where I could help others. Fortunately, I had experience going to Nicaragua with a group that built homes and fed families in some of the poorest neighborhoods in the world.

Four months into my recovery, I realized I was capable of the travel and the service work and signed up for the trip. It was extraordinary. We built 3 basic homes and purchased 2 months' worth of food for more than 150 families in an impoverished neighborhood called Tipitapa in Managua, Nicaragua.

It was great to see the smiles of the kids, hear the laughter and every "Thank you," and see the tears of the families who had newly built homes. It was spectacular.

At that point in my recovery, I was healthy enough to go, but I was still cautious, making sure I had my supplements and plenty of food and that I stayed hydrated.

The service you choose does not have to be so extreme. It can be closer to home. For example, two months into my PCS, I asked my girlfriend out to dinner for Valentine's Day. During the day leading up to our date, I had several breakdowns, so I called her and canceled.

Not wanting to disappoint her too much, I went to her house with two dozen roses. One dozen was for her, and the other dozen were for some other special people who did not have the good fortune of having someone to share Valentine's Day with.

My girlfriend and I went to a senior living facility in North Scottsdale, approached the front desk, and asked if we could deliver a single rose to 12 different people.

They said, "Absolutely!" and we proceeded to give that little gift to some lonely people. Even with my brain injury, I was able to serve, and that service made my life a little better. I encourage you, if you're suffering, to get involved in a small service project, and see if that helps. Remember, always consult your doctor before doing anything.

Bonus Step!

There's one last step that I would like to share with you, which I believe had a role in my recovery: my intensive session with a technology called Brain State. They call it "brain wave optimization." I did their five-day intensive at their headquarters in Scottsdale, Arizona, which included two sessions per day over five days, one in the morning and one in the afternoon.

The Brain State technology uses EEG brain readings and audio bio feedback from their software program. I'm not sure of the science behind it, but four months into my recovery, I found it to be very helpful. In fact, after day five, I felt like I was back to my old self! I had replaced my negative, anxious thoughts with powerful, creative thoughts.

Their assessment report showed that my temporal lobes were not in sync (my terminology, not theirs), which left my brain in a constant state of fight or flight. This drained my brain of much-needed energy because it was always on the lookout for a constant threat, which is typical for concussion survivors.

Bonus Step #2

One of the greatest pieces of advice I received came from my friend Tana Amen when she said, "Kevin, recovery is not a straight line. The brain is very complex, and as you recover, you may experience dips and setbacks. Just know that those are normal."

Thank God Tana told me that because it is true! There were times when I made significant progress only to have a sudden anxiety attack that would send me into a bit of an emotional spiral. That advice saved me!

I am grateful to report that as of writing this, almost exactly three years after my accident, I am happy, healthy, and back to myself—hopefully even better. There are times when I struggle with simple memory issues, which could be a result of my brain injury, but it does not stop me from living a powerful life. I continue to pursue a healthy lifestyle and an interest in improving my brain.

I've connected with some of the top doctors, professionals, and others involved in the world of brain injuries. I recently spent time at the Amen Clinics in Costa Mesa, California, where I had my brain scanned using the SPEC technology. I was also able to observe the pioneer in functional neurology, Dr. Ted Carrick, in his office in Marietta, Georgia while he worked on some of the more difficult cases in the world. I recently attended the International Symposium on Clinical Neuroscience, where surgeons, nutritionists, chiropractors, and others spoke on the topic of traumatic brain injuries and neurodegenerative diseases. I'm staying plugged into the community for my own health and so that I can continue to bring you more information from the frontlines of brain injury and recovery.

If you would like to plug into the community that we are building of concussion survivors and their families, please visit The Concussion Recovery Network at www.concusionrecoverynetwork.com, or interact with our Facebook family at www.facebook.com/concussionrecovery.

We would love to hear your story of struggle and triumph. We want to bring this struggle and suffering out of the darkness and into the light for millions of others like us. There is no need to suffer alone.

The Recovery Journal: 3 minutes per day for 30 days can transform your life!

Now that you know my story and you know it's possible to overcome the tragedy of a concussion and create a life that you love, it's time to create a practice of gratitude and love. It's important to do your best to keep a positive outlook during your recovery, even though I know how difficult it can be at times. Having faith that you will have a great outcome can help immensely. So I've designed and included a very simple strategy to help you shift your thoughts. Even if it's for just a few minutes a day, you will benefit. I've included a step by step 30-day guided journal with positive quotes each day to help you get through your tough time and on a road to recovery.

What to do: Use this journal to create a positive shift in your thoughts to help you recover from any personal tragedy. Take 3 minutes per day and simply write 1 thing you are grateful for, 1 person you love, and 1 thing you feel good about today. That's it! It's that simple. You can add more if you'd like, but if you simply think of 1 and write 1, for each category, that will work.

Why do it? Focusing on what we are thankful for and the loved ones in our lives can shift negative patterns very quickly. Done once in the morning and before bed over a period of 30 days can help us not only get through the hard times, but often remind us during the day that we are not alone and that there is hope. Focusing on gratitude and love can also create positive patterns and habits for our brain and we can reap rewards in our lives.

How to do it? There is no exact science to this, it's yours to try out and see what works best for you. Start with filling out the journal in the morning when you first wake up, then keep it by your bed so you can do it again at night before falling asleep. If it causes you stress... put it down for another day. It should take you no more than 3 minutes at a time.

Where to do it? Anywhere you like! We suggest you keep it next to your bed and do it first thing in the morning and/or before you go to bed at night.

Helpful Hint: Find someone in your life who will do it with you if you can. Sharing these things with another person can be valuable to you and the person you are sharing with. Choose a family member, a friend or anyone you feel good sharing with. This isn't necessary to do, but it can be helpful and have someone to rely on in case you forget.

"The journey of a thousand miles begins with a single step." –Lao Tzu

Day 1:

What are you grateful for?

Who in your life do you love?

What will you do today that will make you feel good?

"Let us always meet each other with a smile, for a smile is the beginning of love."- Mother Teresa

Day 2:

What are you grateful for?

Who in your life do you love?

What will you do today that will make you feel good?

"Your success and happiness lies in you. Resolve to keep happy and you shall for an invincible host against a host of difficulties." – *Helen Keller*

Day 3:

What are you grateful for?

Who in your life do you love?

What will you do today that will make you feel good?

"You don't have to see the whole staircase, just take the first step."- Dr. Martin Luther King

Day 4:

What are you grateful for?

Who in your life do you love?

What will you do today that will make you feel good?

"Success is not final. Failure is not fatal. It's the courage to continue that counts."-Winston Churchill

Day 5:

What are you grateful for?

Who in your life do you love?

What will you do today that will make you feel good?

"Once you choose HOPE anything's possible."
-Christopher Reeve

Day 6:

What are you grateful for?

Who in your life do you love?

What will you do today that will make you feel good?

"I can't change the direction of the wind, but I can adjust my sails to always reach my destination." –Jimmy Dean

Day 7:

What are you grateful for?

Who in your life do you love?

What will you do today that will make you feel good?

"There is always a light at the end of each tunnel, but it is only visible and obtainable to those who wish to see it." – unknown author

Day 8:

What are you grateful for?

Who in your life do you love?

What will you do today that will make you feel good?

"Success is to be measured not so much by the position that one has reached in life as by the obstacles which he (or she) has overcome" – Unknown author

Day 9:

What are you grateful for?

Who in your life do you love?

What will you do today that will make you feel good?

"Happiness is not a station you arrive at, but a manner of traveling." -Margaret B. Runbeck

Day 10:

What are you grateful for?

Who in your life do you love?

What will you do today that will make you feel good?

"Most of the important things in the world have been accomplished by people who have kept on trying when there seemed to be no hope at all."
- Dale Carnegie

Day 11:

What are you grateful for?

Who in your life do you love?

What will you do today that will make you feel good?

"If you're going through hell, keep on going." - Winston Churchill

Day 12:

What are you grateful for?

Who in your life do you love?

What will you do today that will make you feel good?

"People often say that motivation doesn't last. Well, neither does bathing – that's why we recommend it daily." - Zig Ziglar

Day 13:

What are you grateful for?

Who in your life do you love?

What will you do today that will make you feel good?

"Many of life's failures are people who did not realize how close they were to success when they gave up."- Thomas Edison

Day 14:

What are you grateful for?

Who in your life do you love?

What will you do today that will make you feel good?

"Our greatest glory is not in never falling, but in getting up every time we fall."- Confucius

Day 15:

What are you grateful for?

Who in your life do you love?

What will you do today that will make you feel good?

"Even in hardship, God's goodness prevails." - Todd Stocker

Day16:

What are you grateful for?

Who in your life do you love?

What will you do today that will make you feel good?

"The most beautiful people I've known are those who have known trials, have known struggles, have known loss, and have found their way out of the depths." — *Elisabeth Kübler-Ross*

Day 17:

What are you grateful for?

Who in your life do you love?

What will you do today that will make you feel good?

"The greater the obstacle, the more glory in overcoming it." – Moliere

Day 18:

What are you grateful for?

Who in your life do you love?

What will you do today that will make you feel good?

"You may encounter many defeats, but you must not be defeated. In fact, it may be necessary to encounter the defeats, so you can know who you are, what you can rise from, how you can still come out of it." – Maya Angelou

Day 19:

What are you grateful for?

Who in your life do you love?

What will you do today that will make you feel good?

"The brick walls are there for a reason. The brick walls are not there to keep us out. The brick walls are there to give us a chance to show how badly we want something. Because the brick walls are there to stop the people who don't want it badly enough. They're there to stop the other people." – Randy Pausch

Day 20:

What are you grateful for?

Who in your life do you love?

What will you do today that will make you feel good?

Always bear in mind that your own resolution to success is more important than any other one thing. -Abraham Lincoln

Day 21:

What are you grateful for?

Who in your life do you love?

What will you do today that will make you feel good?

"Believe you can and you're halfway there." -
Theodore Roosevelt

Day 22:

What are you grateful for?

Who in your life do you love?

What will you do today that will make you feel
good?

"I hated every minute of training, but I said, 'Don't quit. Suffer now and live the rest of your life as a champion." -Muhammad Ali

Day 23:

What are you grateful for?

Who in your life do you love?

What will you do today that will make you feel good?

"A problem is a chance for you to do your best." – Duke Ellington

Day 24:

What are you grateful for?

Who in your life do you love?

What will you do today that will make you feel good?

"The difference between stumbling blocks and stepping stones is how you use them." – Unknown author

Day 25:

What are you grateful for?

Who in your life do you love?

What will you do today that will make you feel good?

"Tough times never last, but tough people do."
– Robert H Schulle

Day 26:

What are you grateful for?

Who in your life do you love?

What will you do today that will make you feel good?

"Believe that life is worth living and your belief will help create the fact." – William James

Day 27:

What are you grateful for?

Who in your life do you love?

What will you do today that will make you feel good?

"Things turn out the best for the people who make the best of the way things turn out." - John Wooden

Day 28:

What are you grateful for?

Who in your life do you love?

What will you do today that will make you feel good?

"I ask not for a lighter burden, but for broader shoulders." – Jewish Proverb

Day 29:

What are you grateful for?

Who in your life do you love?

What will you do today that will make you feel good?

"We must embrace pain and burn it as fuel for our journey." – Kenji Miyazawa

Day 30:

What are you grateful for?

Who in your life do you love?

What will you do today that will make you feel good?

Additional Resources

Here are some additional resource that I found to be helpful in my recovery and that you might find to be helpful too. None of these are meant to replace your medical professional but may add additional insights to your recovery.

Concussion Recovery Network: www.concussionrecoverynetwork.com

Brain State: www.brainstatetech.com

Z-Health: www.zhealth.net

Amen Clinics: www.amenclinics.com

Plasticity Brain Center: www.plasticitybraincenters.com

Carrick Institute: www.carrickinstitute.com

Book: *Change Your Brain, Change Your Life* by Dr. Daniel Amen

Book: *Living the Invisible Disability* by Hannah Andrusky

Movie: *Crash Reel* (documentary)

Movie: *Concussion* (based on a true story)

I sincerely hope you found this special report helpful and that you or your loved one finds healing in your lives. Concussions left untreated can be extremely destructive to the lives of those suffering and to their loved ones. The brain is still a fantastic mystery and an area that deserves much exploration and understanding. What we do know is that it is the control center for our lives. It controls every aspect of our health, emotions, and motor skills. The slightest injury can cause chaos, no matter the age of the injured.

The good news is that there is hope! There is the possibility of healing and recovery, whether you are a young child who has suffered a concussion in a soccer or football game or you are a soldier concussed from the trials of battle.

If you found this report helpful and you know of anyone who is suffering, please share this with them. It is *free* to download at www.concussionrecoverynetwork.com. If you have remedies and resources that have helped you, please share them on the Concussion Recovery Facebook Fan Page:
www.Facebook.com/ConcussionRecovery/
or email us at
info@concussionrecoverynetwork.com. You may also follow us on:

Instagram: @concussionrecoverynetwork

Twitter: @concussionRN

About the Author:

Kevin Donahue is an entrepreneur, author, speaker, and transformational leader. Kevin's concussion recovery has lead him on a mission to find remedies and the latest technologies to help heal those who suffer, as well as bring awareness to the cause.